Looking Under Things To Get Over Them

True accounts of subconscious inquiry

Joanne L. Gartner Ph.D

Contents

Acknowledgements

I wish to salute my brave clients who dive unafraid into themselves to come out with a greater understanding of their lives, a deeper appreciation for the human journey, and sometimes, they tell me, a glimpse of their eternal spirit.

Thanks also to Clyde B. Harvey, my grandmother, who painted the blue swirl which I used for the front cover art.

Introduction

Hypnotherapy is one of many ways available to help you get in touch with more of yourself. I particularly like it because the information you receive is not anyone else's interpretation — not your mother's, your spouse's, your therapist's, your pastor's. It's you talking to yourself in a state of mind you typically already use several times a day. In fact, I don't even hypnotize you. You actually do the hypnotizing, in that you allow yourself to experience the process.

Pardon me, I should say processes, because there is more than one, and often they are not discrete but can flow into one another. People have told me they didn't know they could ask the subconscious questions, but thought they could only tell it what they want. True, the most general and commonly understood methods of hypnotherapy reframe problematic patterns you're holding onto by *telling* your subconscious what goals you want to prioritize in your life today.

If you want to lose your fear of spiders, have a more commanding presence at work, quit smoking, lose weight, meet people, not let Aunt Matilda get to you at family gatherings, whatever else — then we, you and I together, tell the subconscious what you consciously choose to be different in your life. This works well when you know what behavioral changes you want to make in order to better deal with things that trigger you negatively or even to simply fast forward your goals.

Also, however, you can learn the reasons for patterns and problems in your life by *asking* your subconscious for information. And you can ask for solutions. Some clients are so overwhelmed with situations, opinions, and choices, they aren't sure which way to turn — or feel they don't have any choices at all. They may just want to know their next best step, or they may want to understand underlying causes for specific challenges they are currently facing. This is when I put on my seatbelt because I never know where the session is going and I'm guaranteed a fascinating experience every time!

This book is a compilation of the results people have received when they've *asked* their subconscious for information — as the title suggests, when they've looked under things to get over them. Of course, all names have been changed.

Please know that entire sessions are not presented here. There is always a more thorough discussion at the beginning to clarify clients' questions than what you'll read here. And there is therapeutic work which follows what you'll read here, to help clients release or reframe feelings and beliefs so that they can go forward more positively. Herein, I'm just giving you an account of the information people have found to lie beneath the surface of their conscious thought.

You need to understand that the subconscious doesn't speak English or any other language. It communicates with imagery instead of words, and the images you get may have any number of different meanings, which are not mine to determine but yours. You may imagine yourself emerging from a cocoon and flying, and because of the incredible confidence you feel when you experience yourself flying, you interpret that as encouraging you to step out and try that something-new you've been thinking about. You may see yourself in a jail cell and realize how much you've pulled away from people, and then consider what it takes to feel safe letting yourself out to reconnect with friends and family. You may get a sense of yourself having moved to the very city you're contemplating moving to and running a successful business there — right down to the details of the products or services you offer, the kinds of clients you serve, and the demographic of employees you hire.

Or you may perceive a scenario where you're a different person altogether, in a completely different time and place — often centuries in the past. Is something like that truly a past-life you are seeing? I don't know; you may decide that for yourself. What I do know is that those experiences can help clients better understand their lives today and can motivate them positively and sometimes very powerfully toward current goals. Even deeply religious people who say their churches don't 'believe' in past-lives have found profound spiritual meaning from what appears in the regression process to be a past life.

Whether a person has had previous regressions or not, it is my observation that they always come out of a session with a sense of awe. The most common result, apart from receiving the specific answer or advice they were seeking, is that folks tend to take a more relaxed view of things happening in their lives now, so they feel less bothered by other people's foibles. My own awe as a therapist is for the consistent ability of a person's subconscious to help with what he or she needs at that particular time.

The only client I've had who has not been satisfied with a session asking for information was a gentlemen who danced around his issue awhile and when he got to the difficult, core question said, "I really don't want to know." At that point, I simply switched to the more traditional *telling* hypnotherapy to anchor the goal he'd clarified that he wanted. No harm, no foul.

Whatever path you choose to get in touch with more of yourself, may you come to know you're a powerful being, may you be kind to yourself on your journey of learning and growth which inevitably includes mistakes and misunderstandings, and may you see the beauty and value that is uniquely yours simply for being YOU.

Seeing Things More Clearly

Often clients are better able to see issues and uncover connections by reviewing circumstances when they are more relaxed — not necessarily even in trance, but very relaxed. With the logical, problem-solving part of their mind on the back burner, so to speak, their thinking more easily brings up what it is they need to be aware of. They may describe the same events they would have depicted ordinarily, but once their brain-waves slow down there is often a different emphasis, a little different perspective, or just the calmness needed to let some aspect sink in.

Dreams are also interesting in the way they reflect information to us. All elements of a dream have meaning and even other people in our dreams have to do with something about ourselves. We often know when a dream is trying to tell us something important; sometimes we just need a little help figuring it out.

Lily and the Energy Loop

*L*ily was a sole business owner and single mother with no custodial support. She was also closely involved with her family both by helping those who were local to her and traveling regularly to those who lived out of state. Lily's relationship with her mother, Wendy, was chronically difficult, exacerbated by the fact that Wendy was heavily dependent upon others, and this stained with envy the pride she had for her independent daughter.

This particular year Lily's business income suffered an usually low seasonal dip, and she had no recourse except to move herself and her son back in with her parents for a few months. The arrangement was highly beneficial for her parents, because of the money Lily was able to contribute to the household as well as the help she provided to take care of her grandmother.

Yet despite the advantages of having Lily in her home and stating that she was welcome there, Wendy took time almost daily to remind Lily of the practical adjustments it cost her to endure, the alarming rise in electric consumption (even though Lily was paying more than the increase for her share of the utilities), how great was her own contribution to helping Lily raise her son, etc.

Lily well understood her mother's martyrdom — after all she'd been dealing with it for decades — but she couldn't prevent getting caught up in it and found herself regularly hurt and frustrated to the point of tears. In a relaxed state, Lily was able to succinctly reveal the core difficulty of their dynamic.

She just won't leave me alone! She has to knit-pick about things that don't matter, things that I'm paying for and don't cost her anything, things that have nothing to do with anything. She has to push her "sacrifices" on me and try to control me, but I've got to where I can take away her power.

I remind her how something she says is the exact opposite of what she said the day before; I go into great detail about how I'm doing the things she previously wanted so what's happened now is simply a logical result; I use her own thinking against her. I'm able to take her power away but still, she has to come into my room and nyah-nyah-nyah-nyah-nyah-nyah-nyah-nyah-nyah. She just has to give me such a hard time!

So Wendy gave and Lily took — therein lay the power cycle. As much as Lily took Wendy's power away as a way to protect herself, Wendy kept rebuilding it and giving it back as a way of protecting *herself*. Whereas some people have a tug-of-war struggle where the direction of the impulse stops and reverses itself, these two had a flow that could accelerate unimpeded, fed by the momentum they each provided. The irony was that each was acting in a way that she thought would stop it, but effectively fueled the energy of the loop and increased the tension rather than decreasing it.

Giselle in Pirate Waters

*A*n intelligent and intuitive woman in her mid-30s, Giselle came in because she was stymied that she could not move forward. "It's like I'm stuck. I used to be so confident in myself, sure of my future, and bold with my decisions. Now it's like I don't know who to trust or what to believe. I can't get past my uncertainty and make decisions."

It turns out that Giselle had been on vacation in SE Asia seven years earlier with a friend, and they were part of a small group taking a half-day boat ride out to an island. She'd called her parents to say her cell phone would likely not receive a signal, and not to expect to hear from her for a week or so. She'd had some foreboding about the trip, but her friend talked her out of it.

The engine broke down; they had little food and no radio. They ended up being adrift at sea for 3 days in waters known to have pirate activity, so people would wave but kept their distance — no other boat would approach close enough to see that they were broken down. No one's cell phone had a signal and after a day their power was gone anyway. She knew her parents wouldn't worry because they expected not to hear from her.

And there was a bad storm — a 20-ft boat weathering 10-ft waves. *It was so terrible! I prayed when we dipped into a wall of water that the men standing on the out-riggers to balance the boat would still be there. They were so brave; I prayed so hard...* She was nearly sobbing.

First was the deep anger at herself for not heeding the apprehension she'd clearly experienced before the trip.

I was so MAD at myself, I felt like I only had myself to blame for not speaking up because I didn't listen to that inner warning.

Second was the unremitting terror of realizing they had no means to get back to land against the currents, of worrying hour after hour, day after day, that no one would stop to help them, and of dreading they might capsize.

We didn't feel hungry because we were so full of fear, not knowing if anyone was ever going to help us. All our energy went into looking and looking and looking out over the water. It was such a gnawing dread, I can't describe it — it just, it was just so awful.

Third was a whole new anxiety, after some people finally did tow them back to land.

A group of people came forward to help us, and then another group would accuse them of being kidnappers. And the first group would say, "no, they're the ones who'll kidnap you, not us!" It was impossible to tell. We didn't know who to believe!

Hence almost two more days' wait for a navy ship — not a U.S. Navy ship, but the local country's navy ship. And then the stressful suspicion of being separated for questioning, having to be proven innocent themselves of possible criminal activity out on the open ocean in a foreign country.

At the time, she'd dealt with this as best she could; and at the time, that was likely adequate. But here she was in my office seven years later saying she felt stuck and indecisive, unsure what to believe and who to trust, couldn't seem to face her future with courage, and didn't have the confidence in herself that she'd had when she was younger.

Giselle hadn't previously connected her current obstacles with this experience. As she reviewed the details of the ordeal, she saw the connection.

You know, it's like I never really got off that boat!

Kamal and the Car

Kamal had a dream that she couldn't get off her mind, so she felt it was something she was supposed to pay attention to. She'd dreamt that she was driving and her car broke down out in the country near an abandoned garage. Although it made no sense logically, she also had brought a second car there with her.

So I decided to leave the broken car in the garage, I knew it would be safe there, that no one would bother it and no one would mind. And I could go on with the second car.

Then some time later, I found myself back at the garage again and needed something to drive — it wasn't that anything had happened to the second car, I just didn't have it at the time. I knew I could get the broken car out of the garage. I realized it really only needed a jump start and would be fine.

Once she was relaxed, she could better see that in the dream she'd actually taken the time to consider each decision several times: first that the broken car would be safe in the garage, and second that it would be drivable with just a battery boost, so she could go safely on in it.

I asked her, "Is there something you've sort of... put away for a while?"

Kamal thought for a moment. *What do you mean?*

"Well, like maybe a project you shelved, and now feel ready to consider taking up again...?"

(Pause) *Oh my gosh, I think it's a friend that I was getting a little tired of! We've been friends for a long time, but she was sort of bugging me, and I just haven't seen her as often now for some time. I guess I'm ready to spend more time with her again, and making that decision several times, that it would be OK to use the broken car — I think that means that yes, this is a good time to pick that friendship back up. It's been in the back of my mind lately, whether or not to get back on track with her like before.*

"And who or what might the second car represent?"

Well, that would probably be another friend I've had much longer — she's always there for me, ever since high school.

"And what could the garage represent?"

Let's see, the garage was abandoned but not run-down — and it wasn't like I felt I was trespassing or anything, it was just conveniently available. So that feels like putting my friend away a while would not jeopardize our relationship in the long run, that she would be safe there.

Oh, I get it, that our relationship would be OK! And that this IS a good time to start back up again. Do you think it means anything that it was out in the country, where there was nothing around?

"What does that being-out-in-the country tell you it means? Ask yourself…"

Mmmmm… that there was not enough in the relationship at the time, 'nothing around it,' and that's where it broke down.

It all makes so much sense now. Wow, that's crazy!

Roxanne's Eye on Herself

Roxanne's dream had her completely puzzled; it occurred in three segments. First was needing to choose between an eye in a red circle, reminiscent of eye shadow, and something else unknown. The feeling she had at the time was that the unknown was the better choice.

Second was a song:

"I was born in the morning,

An eye above Venus.

She didn't seem to think about it,

Why should you?"

Third was an admonition: UNDERSTAND YOUR BANNER.

After she was relaxed, I asked what stood out the most for her.

Well, there's an eye in both the first and second parts.

"What may that mean to you, an eye? And maybe not what an eye means all the time, but here in your dream?"

Well, here they feel like they're watching, keeping an eye on things...

"Is that a good watching or an ominous watching? Who's doing the watching?"

Oh it's me watching. It feels like I'm doing it... for myself, actually. It's for my own good.

"And you opted for the unknown instead of the eye in the red circle because...?"

Mmmmm... because the eye in the red circle is already what I know, and I need to move into the unknown. I need to do things that are different. The red-circle eye will help keep me straight, it's watching out for me, as I step out of what I know.

"OK. Now how about the song, what stands out there?"

Oh, the eye is above Venus! Venus is feminine power, intuition...

(Pause) A few years ago, a psychic told me that I once lived in a female-dominant culture that did sacrifices. I didn't know what I was getting into by being involved with that, and that's why in this life now I want to stay on the straight and narrow. She said I have very high walls up to not use my intuition.

So I think it means it's OK for me now to step into my intuition because I'll be keeping an eye on myself to do good and not do harm! Choosing the red-circle eye in the first part would mean staying where I was, being safe, but I'm nudging myself to step in the unknown and this time I will keep an eye on doing good things and not bad. I'll have an eye on myself!

"And the rest of the song?"

Those parts just support that I can start to use my intuition, like the dawning of it, and it won't be a problem. As the essence of that power, Venus isn't worried about me misusing it.

"Now the only part left is the banner."

That's easy to figure out now: the banner is to stay with what I stand for, to keep myself in integrity.

"So how does all that feel?"

It feels great, very self-affirming because I'm starting to take a greater interest in expanding my consciousness and becoming more aware, which means using more intuition. And this is me giving myself permission!

Finding Personality Roots

People often find traces of skills and interests reflected in situations that clearly present themselves as past-life experiences. It is said that if you want to know where and when you may have lived in the past, look at your life today. What does your décor reflect? What types of foods do you like (or not like!)? What about your clothes styles…? What cultures and places and eras are you drawn to or averse to? You'll get inklings!

Thomas's Rattles

homas was between jobs and wasn't sure where to turn next. Currently, he found himself interested in herbs, essential oils, and crystals, and was wondering where these might lead.

In regression, he saw himself in clothes hand-made from animal skins, living in the woods somewhere in Eastern Europe in a tribal community. He used a fairly large rattle from which hung a cord tied with crystals and feathers to collect and release energy, and was looked up to as a medicine man!

I heal people and read energy. I can step into non-physical dimensions, meet energy beings, and get messages about healing from spirit guides and plants. Then I teach others in my tribe. The more I teach others, the more I am able to learn myself — I feel like if I kept it to myself, then the channel would, I don't know, I guess it would shut down. It's important to share the information.

He saw himself in the middle of a large ceremony to celebrate the time of harvest. The men and women of his tribe were dancing in a circle, while he held the energy and drummed the rhythm for them.

It's not religious; it's just our way of relating to the environment, to nature. Everyone uses their energies to communicate, asking for help from nature's spirits to heal each other and to experience prosperity in everyday activities. We all learn from an early age to use energy and anyone who doesn't do it for positive purposes gets more intense tutoring, not punishment.

Thomas felt very connected to this group of people and looked back to notice how he accepted more and more responsibility as he'd grown older. By young adulthood, he was half student with a medicine man older than he and half teacher with a younger person who was in training to learn deeper energy work. Some of the people in his tribe there were friends in his current life now — notably his sister, one of his best friends, and a nephew.

The message he came away with, like others who have had similar regression experiences, was a sense that there is a lot of power and wisdom he can access and reconnect with, and that he can feel safe and confident to let it unfold without doubting it.

Out of regression, Thomas mentioned that he already had a collection of rattles, and now he was going to start tying cords on them like the one in his regression. He was also eager to investigate energy work and see how he felt about it. He'd thought about it before but couldn't decide, and now was confident that he would easily recognize which type of healing practice would be right for him.

Josie's Teacher Past

*J*osie, an educator for decades, told me she had a friend who'd seen her in a dream as a Native American woman high up a cliff on a ledge that led into a cave — and that she was sweeping the ledge and gesticulating to some plants. So Josie decided to see for herself if that was a past life.

In trance, she saw where she'd been a Native American, living high up a cliff in a cave by herself, apart from the others.

I would teach young women the tribal lore and traditions, and also the men who were being primed to become chiefs. They would come to my cave to learn. But as the tribe became more westernized, the older ways were left behind, and fewer and fewer came to learn.

There had been a daughter, but it was unclear if the girl had died or simply moved away. Furs draped the walls, and she could see that by overlapping them she was able to keep out the cold winter wind.

I could lay down on the ledge with my arm in front of my face so my eyes just peeped over it. I was far enough away that I could watch people down below and if I did not move, they wouldn't know I was there. It feels like the tribe maybe moved on, and I stayed behind. For sure, I was left behind because they did not keep the old ways alive.

Just at the end of the session, Josie heard, "SHE DECORATED THE CAVE WITH THINGS THAT PEOPLE COULD NOT SEE. At the time, she wasn't sure what this meant. A few days later, she was laughing to realize she'd already been creating things people couldn't see. Some time ago she'd imagined a big pyramid over her house, the Pyramid of Protection. And more recently she'd invented the Cone of Happiness inside her home, to remind herself to recapitulate each day and let go of negative feelings, so that she would go to sleep untroubled.

After noticing the Pyramid of Protection and Cone of Happiness as parallel types of events, Josie revisited the Native American woman on her own to learn what invisible things she'd decorated the cave with. This is how information continues to unfold for clients, as they connect the regression experience to what's happening in their lives today.

Carrying Emotions

Our subconscious can hold onto emotional imprints for years and we're not even aware they continue to affect us. Interesting, too, is that before the age of about seven, we absorb impressions without filters, so fears and biases can lodge in our subconscious that aren't even related to our own direct experience.

The regression process may go back to an earlier point in this life, to when we were being delivered or even in the womb, to past lives, or to times between lives. Those experiences can explain the presence of people and patterns of behavior in our current lives, because the emotional charge we have attached to someone or something has carried over to today.

Hannah in France

Hannah had witnessed a person on fire and was looking for a way to help her get over that. She and several other people had ripped off their jackets to help put out the flames and no one wanted to leave him until the emergency medical team arrived. He did not survive the night and many of the people there shared a special bond from the experience. She was now looking for more than the comfort of camaraderie; she was looking for a deeper solution to heal her recurring thoughts.

In regression, Hannah found herself a very young woman speaking to crowds of French villagers in the Middle Ages. She would go from town to town attempting to recruit people, usually men, to join her in battle.

I wasn't Joan of Arc, but I think there were other girls who were inspired to be like her, and I was one of them. It doesn't seem like I really caused much trouble but I was recalcitrant and they felt they had to make an example of me. They didn't want more of that popping up, and...

Oh God, they burned me at the stake. Yes, that's what happened!

"OK, you're safe now. You don't need to relive that. Just see it like on a TV screen or we can stop."

No, it's OK. I'm OK. I think I just didn't believe it would come to that... Such mean people. But I was so stubborn!

No wonder I hate everything French. I never had a reason, I just have always felt repulsed by anything to do with France.

Hannah believed that witnessing the man on fire had triggered this buried past-life memory, and now that the reason for it was uncovered, she would be able to better put it behind her. Out of regression, she recalled, "You know, in 7th grade I dressed as Joan of Arc for costume day!"

Six months later she was taking a French class and loving it. She even had plans to go to France the next summer, said she could hardly wait!

Nick's Shame

Nick came in feeling conflicted because all of the feedback he got at work was complimentary and indicated absolute success, whereas his internal state was one of shame and inadequacy. He was chronically worried he was going to be let go and some of his coworkers had begun to think he was fishing for complements, when in fact his self-doubt was very real.

In regression, he found himself in some kind of a bubble, able to hear voices but unable to see beyond the space he was in.

Actually I can't really see anything. But it's very familiar so I just know what's around me; I'm comfortable here.

"Are you alone?"

There are others, but not in my space here.

"Do you ever talk to them?"

Not really. I know they're there, and they know I'm here. It's like that's enough.

"How do you feel about not talking with them?"

Well, some I want to talk to. Others I want to go away.

"Why is that?"

Because they're... I guess I'd have to say they're mean."

"To you?"

Sort of to me, but not really. I can't really describe it; I just feel what they're like.

"And what is the message for you, here in this bubble?"

It's that I have to be careful, careful, careful. They can be mean anytime. It's like I don't know when it will happen. I just have to be so careful.

From furthering questioning, it turned out that when Nick's mother was pregnant with him, she had a new job and made a mistake. It wasn't actually a big mistake, but she had been embarrassed and teased, and then never allowed herself to be relaxed around her coworkers there. She remained always on guard against what she saw as their ever-ready ridicule.

Nick came to see that he had taken on his mother's emotional wariness and carried it all this time — he had never had an experience of his own to warrant the shame!

Eric in Jail

Twenty-seven-year-old Eric wanted to know if a regression might reveal the cause for his being a chronic nail-biter, which was not such a big deal when he was young, but caused him frustration and embarrassment as he became older.

In regression, he found himself as a young man trekking across a desert to a small town, in a time long before modern transportation when people either walked or rode horses.

My clothes are basically a type of robe, like brown homespun. The town is a bunch of short brown buildings, like clay, and all the streets lead into to a central area, like the spokes of a wheel.

He noted a particular doorway as he passed that he knew he would be coming back to, but for now proceeded to the town center. Several people there were watching the only color that appeared in the otherwise brown scene — a jester of sorts in black and white on a small stage, performing cartwheels and other acrobatics for entertainment.

I don't know why, but I don't want to go out into the open. I'm not hiding exactly but I don't particularly want to be noticed.

So he leaned against a building at the edge of the town square with a good view of the open common area, watching the people who were watching the jester. Suddenly several men in uniforms on horseback charged out from one of the streets on the opposite side of the square, and everyone scattered in fear — it was apparent they were looking for someone!

I think it's me they're looking for! I'm pretty sure it's me but I don't know why...

Thankful he was not out in the square where he would have been seen, Eric retreated hastily back up the street he'd come down and knocked anxiously on the door he noticed before.

An old woman opened the door and nervously looked to see that I was not followed then quickly motioned me in. It was awkward, I had to step down from the street level into the building and be careful not to bang my head. She gave me a ring and seemed to want me to leave right away — no friendly chit-chat. Just sort of, 'here you go, good-bye!'

It was a signet ring like royalty used to seal official documents with hot wax, and whoever was in possession of it would wield significant power.

Losing no time to get out of town, Eric walked back across the desert expanse to a bigger city with grander buildings, elaborate landscaping, and wide avenues. His heart leapt as he looked over to his right.

I'm passing by my house, it has a white picket fence, where I live now with a woman and her daughter, we're becoming a family and very happy together. That's where I'll go after I deliver the ring.

As he approached a palatial building with steps wide enough that several carriages could park in front of them, a well-dressed man in stately garb descended to meet him and surreptitiously accepted the ring. Eric was pleased to have restored it to the person he felt was its rightful owner. He did not anticipate compensation for his efforts, as the satisfaction for doing a good deed was reward enough.

To his complete astonishment and confusion, he was thrown into a prison cell and no one returned for him — ever. He was not fed or cared for in any way. There was no one else in his cell or in any other cell around him; he was utterly alone. Believing a grave mistake had been made and that surely someone would come back with an apology or explanation, Eric desperately tried to stay alive. He feared the woman he lived with would think he'd run away and she might never learn the truth.

I was so frantic and upset, but just got weaker and weaker. I ate my nails and calloused skin, even licked myself to try and stay clean, but no one ever came back for me — no one ever came, I died there.

As a result of this regression, Eric decided he could either bite or not bite his nails, and live without the burden of self-recrimination.

Molly, a Step-Mother

Despite understanding the challenges of helping raise a teenager and knowing their relationship was essentially positive at its core, Molly was curious why she and her step-son, Mario, butted heads so regularly — it seemed so unnecessary! She came in seeking information to help her cope with the frustration their confrontations caused her to feel.

In regression, Molly saw herself to be a young Grecian man roughly in the early Middle Ages, descending narrow winding stairs in some kind of stone building to reach a courtyard below.

I'm about 22-23; Mario is my younger brother — he's like 12 or 13. There's some kind of tension between us regarding a woman. I don't know if it's competition for our mother's attention, or that I have a girlfriend and he being a little kid, he thinks she's his girlfriend. And there's something not quite right with his health. I don't know if it's that he's mentally slow or maybe has a physical disability.

Oh, he died. It wasn't my fault, but I felt I should have looked after him better, not just seen him as a pesky little brother. I felt pretty bad about that.

From this experience, Molly realized she now had the opportunity as his step-mother to resolve that regret. She found herself taking a larger view of her step-son's peccadilloes, and appreciated more deeply being part of his life.

Janelle and the Money

Janelle had given a man she barely knew a large sum of money to pursue his dream. She respected what he wanted to do with the money and did not regret giving it to him, but questioned if she'd been foolish.

In regression, Janelle saw the two of them standing inside a large ornate tent in a Saharan terrain, rich tapestries hanging from the walls and lush rugs beneath their feet. The man she'd given the money to was her son, a grown man, and they were just looking at each other.

We're saying goodbye, but there are no more words to be spoken. He's going to lead an army on horseback to fight in my honor, and we both know with complete certainty that he will die in the battle. His death will save my life and some modicum of our family honor, otherwise we both would die. He is sacrificing himself for me!

So the monetary gift in this life now allowed him to have the future she felt she'd cost him in the past. Janelle was then able to let go of the fear that she'd made a mistake, wearing instead the satisfaction of knowing she'd done something especially important for another person.

And there is an interesting twist to this regression. Even though she cannot explain why, Janelle is 100% convinced that if she had not given the money open-heartedly to this man with no more reason than that it felt right at the time, then she would never have experienced the tent scene to recall the karmic debt she felt she owed him.

When I probed to understand this further, she replied, "I guess it's that I couldn't be just, 'Oh, OK I owe you this so here you go.' It had to be from my heart without any sense of obligation."

Repeating Patterns

Sometimes people are living out patterns with others that appear to be repetitive lifetime after lifetime, even when their genders and familial relationships change from one timeframe to another. Sometimes we take on different roles to help each other with lessons we need to learn, or deal with unfinished business. The roles we take on may include being the 'bad guy' so that a person we care about will have the experience he or she needs for soul growth.

And now put on *your* seatbelt, because quantum science indicates that outside of this particular experience we are currently in, time is not linear. This means that our 'past' lives are simply 'other' lives — that in fact they are all happening simultaneously. If say, you wanted an experience that you felt would best be achieved in 12th century Spain, you could do that!

This theory would explain the final scenario in this section, which is a progression rather than a regression, meaning that it occurs in the future. The reason more people do not see future-lives is probably because we so heavily subscribe to the mass agreement of linear time here that it is not easily transcended.

Sonya and the Cave

ngaged for few years to a great guy — really, her best friend — Sonya just couldn't make that final step down the aisle and wasn't sure how much longer Viktor would wait. The core of the problem she outlined was that Victor would not live anywhere outside his home state, and she found the prospect of not being able to live other places unbearable — the actual word she used was 'suffocating'. Traveling on vacations would not be enough for her; she needed to experience new places, whereas Viktor was happily ensconced where he was and refused to consider moving.

In regression, the first scenario she found herself facing was in front of a cave that she did not want to enter. Her voice shook with tension, *I'm afraid to go in there. It's just awful, so terrible in there, I just can't go in, it's so horrible…*

I told her, "OK, without going in, can you get a sense of what's in there, that you're afraid of?"

I can't, it's too awful, I... I just can't... I can't bear it...

"That's fine, not to worry — let's go somewhere else."

<hr />

In the second scenario Sonya saw herself as a man returning home from work with big, black, glossy shoes in a suit and hat, sometime in the 1920s. As he lit a cigar, he could hear his wife (who was Viktor) in the kitchen making a drink, a rather common and unremarkable event. The home felt empty.

Sonya, here the husband, was happy with his wife. Viktor, here the wife, was deeply sad that they had no children. She'd lost several children due to miscarriages.

No matter what I tried to do, I couldn't pull her out of her sadness and depression. She became an alcoholic, was addicted to pills, and attempted suicide. She passed away at the age of 45, never was able to get out of the dark, emotional hole she was in.

Standing at her gravesite Sonya was hurt not only that she was gone, but that he hadn't been able to reach her once she'd retreated into her emotional darkness.

Why didn't we try to adopt? There really was no reason for such deep grief; we could have found joy in other things, but she was just so... lost. That life was a waste!

<hr />

35

Next, Sonya saw herself between lives simply as a spirit; other spirits appeared as lights around her — they were souls who all loved one another, spoke endearingly, and shared a deep knowingness. She was profoundly happy, savored that being one big family felt like a warm blanket, and reveled in their connection to God and divine self-power. They were planning their next lives on Earth, even though she wanted to stay there.

I asked, "Then why do you leave and come back here?"

Because what else is there to do when the others go? There are goals and to be with friends is to enjoy more. It's like I don't want to be left behind.

We spoke of how people reincarnate in groups with missions and lessons to work out together, often with friends they enjoy being with and taking on roles to help one another. Then she gasped, *Oh, I see it now! Viktor and I have had lifetimes with sadness and grief, so many of them...*

"OK, let's not worry about all of them; let's go to the very first one and see what happened."

—　～

(Long pause) *It's the cave!*

I even got goose bumps myself — her subconscious had brought her there in the first place, but she didn't want to face it. Would she be able to face it now?

"Alright, without reliving whatever is upsetting, let's just get a sense of what happened there." I reminded her that she was safe now, explained how to keep her emotional distance to witness what happened, and let her know we could stop whenever she felt it was too much to handle.

We died in there, it was so traumatic, our whole family. Our children died, we couldn't keep them alive, and we died in there. It... it was just... so... terrible...

She didn't say if there had been a cave-in or if they had become lost, but it was not quick, and it was deeply disturbing. I had the impression they died with great pain, either emotional or physical or both.

Viktor's... condition... is so rooted. I keep trying to stop the cycle of sadness and fear, but each time the life gets choked out of us. (Although Sonya did not say it, this "choking" may be what happened to them in the cave — her entire account is filled with terms that indicate an inability to breathe. They may have run out of air or succumbed to noxious gases.)

That's why he won't live anywhere else — he's paralyzed emotionally. He feels safe in one place and he won't move. I keep trying to get him out of his shell, lifetime after lifetime, and I can't do it. I waste my life trying over and over. He needs not to be snuffed out. He's all about safety, and I want safety too but I also want joy. His world is so small, it's like I can't breathe in it.

From this, Sonya realized she no longer resented Viktor's stubbornness, because she had a new compassion for where it was coming from. Still, she was likely faced with yet another lifetime of feeling suffocated trying to get him to see a bigger world, or having a different kind of sadness — that of not being with her best friend.

Isaac's Boss/Father

*I*saac had always accepted his father Ben's somewhat over-bearing way of being parental, but he struggled as a well-established and successful adult with Ben's competitiveness and lack of emotional support. He could see that other people received more regard and coopera- tion from his father, and wondered, "Why not me?"

In regression, Isaac saw himself as a teenage fisherman in an Arabic country, where he worked with several others his age for Ben, who was not only his boss but also the owner of the house that his family lived in. Perhaps because Isaac's family would suffer if Isaac attempted to strike out and try other work, or because it was simply his nature, Ben was extremely dismissive of Isaac and took him for granted.

My whole life, I couldn't do anything else, I was so stuck. I liked the fishing, but not the market. And even after I took over running the fishing operation, and all the work at the market, he still treated me like a servant. He felt that the people working under him were indebted and weak-minded. So that's how he saw me, even though I was basically taking care of him at the end, and that never changed.

— —

In another scenario, Isaac saw himself in a dungeon wearing steel handcuffs, thin, barely fed and clothed, middle-aged. He was a poor beggar and had been jailed for stealing food. Ben was his guard, not so mean physically as psychologically, with comments like, "If it weren't for me, you wouldn't have anything at all."

We prisoners became indebted to him simply because there was no one else to care for us; he was the only one who brought food or... anything! It was the only way to get even the least of subsistence, and he lorded it over us.

At this point, Isaac could read that the rapport between himself and Ben was one that had been constructed of so many lives with a more business-like relationship of indebtedness (Isaac always being the debtor), that Ben was unable to overcome that dynamic in the more personal family setting that they were in today. Isaac's challenge was to come up with ways that would help Ben develop a different perspective, and now he understood what that perspective was about.

While still in regression, Isaac asked what he might try doing to improve their relationship, and was surprised at the simple suggestions his subconscious offered that his logical mind had not thought of.

Pam's Divorce

Pam claimed her divorce was proving to be the most difficult experience of her life and wanted to know why it was taking her so long to shake it off, despite having made clear progress over the several years since it had taken place. What she found is testimony to the care we take in setting up lessons for ourselves — three separate lifetimes created the dynamic for her divorce.

In regression, Pam first had a great deal of difficulty 'seeing' where she was, and the entire scenario remained dim throughout.

I think I'm in a small town in the old west. There are dirt streets and the rickety wooden sidewalks. It's so dim, maybe it's dusk? I'm a young man, nothing's happening. I'm just waiting, for who…? I think I'm waiting to meet some people, other men. Oh, that's it — they have work. I'm sort of an iterant ranch hand. I work here and there, so I'm meeting them to find out if they have work for me. Everything seems so slow and it's hard to see.

I have no friends. My 'house' when I'm there is just sort of a one-room shack in the middle of nowhere — I think it's an abandoned shed that I live in when I have nowhere to work. I can't even have a dog because my life is so... shallow, and unpredictable where'll I'll have to go next to get work. It's not living, it's just subsistence. Nothing changes, that's this whole life.

I think the reason it's still dim is because this whole life is dim. It has no depth at all!

Pam got the message of this cowboy life as so devoid of relationships that she ended it wanting more emotional depth.

‒ ‒

Her next scenario was in a fairly opulent courtyard, reminiscent of early Greece inasmuch as she was a young woman in a white, sleeveless, empire-type gown. She was waiting for a young man that she was deeply in love with, and while they were not yet engaged, she believed they soon would be.

Ah, he's the same soul as my ex-husband, but he dies in a carriage accident that day on the way to meet me. He dies before we can be married. It's so devastating. I felt we were cheated, that we were supposed to be together.

Because she never let that feeling go, she carried it over to her current life as a 'debt' that was owed, to be able to be with the person who previously was her soon-to-be affianced, and in this life time became her husband. After the session, Pam expressed a strong intuition that her husband had agreed to be with her in this lifetime, but not with the same commitment — she found out near the end of their marriage that he had been unfaithful to her for most if not all of that time.

— ⁓

In the third setting, Pam saw herself as a monk who lived in a forest well away from civilization. She liked living on her own because she didn't trust people in general and saw them as deceitful.

The lesson from this life is that I wanted to be able to witness deceit and not judge it.

Well, there you have it! First, I wanted to have more emotional depth, and my divorce took me from extreme happiness to the biggest hole of sadness I can imagine. Second, I wanted to be with the personality I wanted to marry, even though we hadn't got to the point of actually being engaged — for all I know, it may be that he never even would have proposed to me. And third, I wanted to be able to witness deceit without judgment — boy, did I get the opportunity to practice that!

I asked her, "Now, if you take a more distanced view, stepping back from your emotions, do you think it's possible that the personality who is your ex-husband may actually be a friend between lives, who agreed to the role of giving you all of these lessons? Even and especially, the emotional depth and the opportunity to witness deceit?"

I'll have to think about that. (Pause) It's probably pretty likely, because I still feel a connection, like I'll catch up with him somewhere else in time, in better circumstances. I just don't want it to be because I'm carrying emotional baggage again!

Martin's Bravery

Martin had suffered vision problems for some time, but due to medical errors, he more recently lost almost all of his sight over a period of a few short months. Adjusting to life as a blind person, especially without the means at hand to be retrained for new employment, was daunting but he got through it. Once his life restabilized, he decided to inquire why this particular obstacle was being put in his path.

In regression, he first saw himself leading a mounted army into battle. It seemed to be a time before guns, as the fight occurred with spears, swords, and arrows.

I'm leading the charge; we have those pennants. I love battle.

"What is it you like about battle?"

It's not for blood-lust. I like being brave, the feeling of being brave against difficulty.

After I no longer fought in battles, I was a… I guess you'd call it a town constable. I would ride around on my horse like a cop on the beat, keeping the peace. But it wasn't the sam; it wasn't satisfying because I didn't have that challenge.

"And what is the message here for your question about the vision problems today?"

Oh, it's that my soul is using the vision challenges as a venue to be brave through. I've outgrown the whole war thing and this is what I'm working with, I think through a few life times, as something to be brave against.

In his next scenario, Martin had difficulty describing where he was.

It's different somehow… like my clothes are transparent… no, maybe translucent. They look like something in the future…? This is like no place on Earth today. Things seem so different. It's quite a ways into the future.

"Can you explain what's different?"

Well, I have different eyes. They're some kind of transplant, and not like human eyes. They go back further on the side of my head, and are made with something organic but it's not human DNA, it's something else. A lot of people are sort of skeptical of this procedure, even of people like me who have these eyes, because we can see things normal human eyes cannot see. It's like different colors and, well… aspects of things.

"Are you treated differently because of your eyes?"

People are just, wary. It's obvious if someone like me has this transplant because these eyes are so much bigger, more elongated. But it's not like discrimination or anything that bad.

"Is your family wary, too?"

No, they're fine with me, because they know me. It's that it's still an oddity; it's not exactly rare to have these, but they're not commonplace, maybe sort of controversial. They make us different, and it's something about the non-human part, I wish I understood it better — sort of like some other species, maybe not even from Earth. It's not just bionic, it's something more organic.

You know, these are really pretty cool! I just don't have the words to describe what it's like, seeing with these.

"And what is the message for you, having these special eye transplants?"

Hmmm. It's that as much as I'm frustrated in this life now, feeling disadvantaged, I won't always be — that in another life I'll be advantaged. It's how things will balance out.

Deepening Faith

I sometimes encounter people who do not 'believe' in past lives, and usually because their church forbids the concept. Fortunately, the gentleman in this section was secure enough in his faith to see what might come forth when he decided to undergo an inquiry.

Another woman's experience was equally elucidative of deepening faith, but she was disinclined to have that regression included here, because she fears her story might be recognized and cause disruption. While she's ceased to speak of it within her congregation, she says her regression experience has been a permanent and positive contribution to her spiritual growth.

Carl in the Ceremonial Room

For personal reasons, Carl was in the position of having a session to ask the subconscious for information, but clarified at the outset that his church did not believe in past lives. We had met twice briefly in different contexts before this, and enjoyed a reasonably comfortable rapport. Nonetheless he was adamant that he had no interest in considering himself in other places in time, wanting to respect and deepen his relationship with the Lord.

I told him that he would be able to hear everything I was saying, so if at any time he was uncomfortable then he could simply tell me he did not want to continue and I would stop the session. On that basis, we began.

In regression, Carl immediately saw himself with curly shoes, elaborate robes, and a turban, somewhere in northern Russia. He was alone in a ceremonial room, unsure why he was there. I asked, "Is this room open to the public?"

No.

"Is it alright for you to be there?"

I think so.

"What are you doing there?"

I don't know.

"What would you like to do there?"

I'd like to give myself to God.

"Well then, why don't you go ahead and do that..."

After about a minute, Carl proceeded to weep softly. I asked if he felt alright.

Yes, I'm alright.

When another couple minutes went by, I advised him that he was not alone; that if he looked around, he would find a friend or relative, an ancestor, a guardian angel, or a spiritual being he would recognize that could help him. He acknowledged that, yes, this was the case, and continued in silence except for sobbing gently from time to time.

Every so often I asked if he wanted to stop and he said, no, that he was fine and wanted to stay there. After almost 15 minutes, he let out a deep sigh and felt he was finished.

After he recovered from being so overwhelmed, I encouraged him to fast-forward to the end of the tur-baned gentleman's life and see how things had turned out for him. Carl then described in halting terms a man so deeply in communion with God that beatific light shone from his face, a man whose connection to the Lord was utterly unshakeable, a man who radiated the most exquisite peace and love.

"And what message does this have for you?"

That I can do this... myself!

Upon coming out of hypnosis, Carl was full of wonder and reverence, you might say like a person who had experienced a kind of transformation. He repeatedly expressed deep gratitude for what he'd seen and felt, surprised that he'd been so guarded about the regression process at the beginning of the session, and realized it did nothing to diminish his faith but instead had meaningfully supported it. He remained in a state of astonishment for some time before he could bring himself to leave.

So I ask you, the reader, to consider whether this was really a past life or if Carl was simply given a vision of insight and motivation. Does it even really matter?

Receiving Information Spontaneously

There is a simple way you can independently become more receptive to subconscious information. It takes advantage of where your mind is when you first wake up, while you're half-awake and half-asleep. This is the same state of mind as hypnosis, and I recommend it for self-hypnosis. Your logical thinking is on the back-burner and your intuitive mind can come to the foreground.

What you do is ask yourself a question at night before you fall asleep. Then when you wake up in the morning, instead of jumping right out of bed, take a few minutes to see what thoughts float up to the surface of your thinking. Be patient, because you may not get an answer right away; it may take days or weeks, but usually if you want information you will get information. And if you respect the process, it will continue and strengthen.

It is common for people to wonder, "Am I making this up?" And once the logical side of your mind begins to wake up, it may start its critique. So just tell it to sit back, that it can have its say-so later after you've had a chance to see what will unfold. Remember, it's just information — if you don't like it, then toss it aside.

What you need to consider about how 'real' the information is, is that of the gazillion combinations of scenarios that you could come up with, why did you come up with the one you did? I believe if you sincerely look at it, you'll begin to find how it can help you.

Once we've opened up to receiving information from the subconscious, it can happen more spontaneously. The sections below are how this happened for me.

My Boss and I in Egypt

Getting a massage one time, I was so relaxed that my mind was just drifting and I began to wonder what my past connections are to ancient Egypt, a time and place I've always been fascinated with.

No sooner had this wondering began, when I felt myself to be a middle-aged man, standing shirtless in a wrapped shendyt on a very wide outdoor platform. To my left were large columns in front of some kind of building and to my right, steps led down to street traffic, mostly people on foot and occasionally on horses. Also to my right sat a younger man on an imposing throne-like chair, facing out toward the street, receiving visitors, and meting out justice for business disputes — the pharaoh!

Immediately upon noticing him, I realized I was his uncle, a trusted advisor. It was my task to supervise the receiving, storage, and distribution of agricultural goods, primarily large amounts of grain or salt, and manufactured goods such as textiles, that were brought to the pharaoh. I forewent having children of my own in order not to incur any kind of familial dispute for my nephew's power, and willingly ate herbs each day, under careful supervision, that would keep me sterile.

When I thought of his family, I realized he had a wife and 2-3 children, whom I knew well and felt affection for, but they seemed to pale in significance because our relationship, his and mine, was based more strongly on our work together. Our lives were largely defined by our political roles.

As I wondered who this pharaoh was, I was surprised to recognize he was the same soul as the woman who was my boss in this lifetime! In fact, she has been my boss three times. Not only is she highly respected for being professionally fair and personally supportive, she lets her people work without undue oversight or micro-management. This woman could assemble an army of staff on short notice because of the numbers of people who would quit their jobs to work for her. So here we were also working together in the past — no surprise, really.

As I wondered *exactly* who this pharaoh was, I saw the letters:

MEMES

Oh, I thought, *that doesn't look very Egyptian; I must be mistaken. I'll bet it's:*

MEMSES (like Ramses, get it?)

The very moment I had that thought, I heard, "No, there's an N."

Oh, so it must be:

MNEMSES (for whatever reason, I thought that looked real Egyptian...)

The next day I decided to search online for Mnemses — no luck. Memses, no luck, Memes, no luck. In frustration I pulled up the entire pharoanic line, and found: Menes. I was supposed to put the N in the middle, without the S!

It gets better. Besides a fascination for Tutankhamen, later in life I became drawn to the Scorpion King, whom I'd never heard of until The Rock, Dwayne Johnson, played him in *The Mummy Returns*. Since then, though, I would drop an entire afternoon's plans at the last minute when a documentary came on TV about the Scorpion King, whose identity is historically disputed.

Menes is credited with uniting Upper and Lower Egypt, and founding the first pharoanic dynasty — hey, I thought, my boss could do that! It also turns out that many of those pharaohs had multiple names. And among Menes' names, which subsequent pharaohs have erased here and there (hence, the dispute), one is Scorpion!

Don't you know I about jumped out of my skin! First to find historic documentation of my musing, and then to have it hit so close my specific interests... Yet it makes sense, the same as I tell my clients: that our current tastes and interests are affected by our strongest memories.

My Friend, Lynne (And What She's Doing On The Other Side)

Lynne had been a best friend for almost 35 years, and for the last several years before she died, we had spoken on the phone 5-6 days a week. She lived in Sacramento; I in Phoenix — we expected to outlive our significant others and be little-old-lady roommates one day.

It came as a complete shock when I heard from Lynne's husband that she passed away from a heart attack the day before. I also spoke with her brother to see how her family was doing. And then I desperately wanted to know that she was alright with... what? With being 'dead'? I knew she wasn't dead, exactly. She still existed, just not here in 3-D, physical reality.

So I called the only person I knew who could contact her. Margaret Selby is a friend of mine and a professional psychic; you can find her at Psychic Readings by Margaret on Facebook or MargaretSelby.com.

"Margaret, I just found out that a friend of mine has passed away unexpectedly — can you get a hold of her and see if she's OK?"

I'm not sure, Joanne. The first week or two — of OUR time, that is — it's sometimes difficult to contact someone who's died.

"Is that because they may be frightened or confused?"

There are all kinds of reasons, but I'll try. I've got some things to do, let me call you back in an hour or so.

When she called back, she was able to tell me Lynne had had no pain whatsoever as she was coming in from the garage to the house. She simply thought she was having a dizzy spell from standing up too quickly, and noticed she couldn't get the door handle to work. Just as she was beginning to realize something was wrong, her (deceased) grandmother came and took her by the hand.

You need to know that Margaret lives 2,000 miles away from me, never met Lynne, hadn't seen me in several years and hadn't spoken to me in many months. Yet she knew the nature of Lynne's husband's recent surgery, that I'd cut my hair, and that the memorial services weren't going to take place for another week — none of which I'd mentioned. Really, she's good!

She says she's about 25 now, that's the age she's comfortable with. She's staying in a grayish-white house with her grandparents for awhile. It has a porch, two or three large trees and a couple other buildings. There's noth-ing she has to do right now — they're just staying there. Her grandmother is young, too, but her grandfather prefers to be about 50. She can't believe her memorial services won't be for a whole 'nother week.

"Doesn't she want to wait around for a week?"

Oh, there's no time on HER side, she's just surprised that YOU all are waiting a week! And she wants to know what'd you do to your HAIR? (Lynne had always laughed that I trimmed my own hair between professional cuts.)

I knew I had to find a way to connect with Lynne because it wasn't going to be reasonable to call Margaret every day. Please know that I do not consider myself any more psychic than the ordinary person — I think I just wanted it so badly and so completely believed it was possi-ble, that I allowed it to happen. And I also believe that the emotional portals between people are wider open when we are in that kind of shock; it's just that most people are in such deep grief they can't take advantage of them.

What I found worked was to scan mentally for her — it was like a cartoonist's drawing of a scent in the air, a tenuous white ribbon undulating right and left as if blow-ing in the breeze, gradually becoming stronger and then opening into a bubble of space, Lynne's space. I would imagine pulling on that ribbon, draw the bubble toward me, and anchor it by envisioning a second white ribbon from me and then using it to tie a bow with Lynne's rib-bon. Then when the communication was over, I mentally untied the ribbons until the next time.

I believe just about any way you choose to use your imagination to do something like this will work. You may want to picture yourself going into a special room and then coming back out, opening a letter and then putting it back in the envelope, or opening a book and then closing it. Or you may even want to try automatic writing; there are plenty of people who do that with deceased loved ones.

I will add that I have learned some shamanic practices, and I set sacred space before these communications — that amounts to calling in protection from nature: the four directions and heaven and earth. I feel better doing this because I don't want to navigate non-ordinary reality without guidance and safety. I don't know what might go wrong; I'm just a very cautious person. It also helps enable me to leave behind the busy-ness of everyday physical life and more easily communicate within the realm of spirit.

⌒　⌒

Here's what I got from Lynne the first time, a few days after the conversation with Margaret when I was in my closet deciding what to pack for the trip to her memorial services. My eye had stopped several times at a colorfully loud hippie-dress. What Lynne had to say didn't come in like a conversation with back and forth questions and answers, but more as a download:

Yes, I do want you to wear that bright 60's dress. If you don't, I won't be mad but I'll be disappointed. You're worried it isn't appropriate, but it's MY funeral!

Right now, I'm just chillin', filtering things that happened in my life. Even the really difficult times were valuable, because they gave me fortitude that I was able to share with my other selves in different timelines. I can now see everything that happened to me without the labels of "good" or "bad," just for what it was.

Another few days later I was in Sacramento, having decided to stay an extra day after Lynne's services. Waking up in the hotel, I was too sleepy to actually get up and call for sacred space, so I just mentally made a circle of protection.

I'm starting to look ahead at what I might want to do next. Joanne, there are so many more choices than just choosing another incarnation or being assigned to someone else as a guide! You can do short-term, tempo-rary help for a person who is undergoing a particularly harsh experience. Say, at the exact time they are being frightened or abused, you can be there with them, and share their space to lend support and strength.

Instead of being just one person's guardian, you can work with many different people who need help. You can choose a specialty, such as betrayal or abandonment, and work across any number of situations at the same time. You can use art, or music, or whatever else you like. There are many, many possibilities.

I envisioned lists with rows and columns, like an Excel sheet — a whole grid of mix-and-match options. It felt like making selections from a menu or choosing the classes you want for a program of study. I knew the choices are more complicated than I could comprehend, but it made sense that the multiverse would be rich with opportunity.

In the same way that an electric burner still emits heat after you turn it off, I sometimes received information from Lynne after I'd untied the white ribbons and let the connection go. About an hour after the above download,

I was returning from my free hotel breakfast, walking in the bright sunshine, and relishing the crisp morning chill. The air was damp as it had recently rained. As I felt a moist breeze cross my face, I heard her say:

Soak up everything, every piece of wind, every drop of light — get something out of every moment, otherwise you've wasted it. Each lifetime is creating a painting and the brush never stops!

I teach with analogies so I loved it: the brush never stops! We don't need to do anything in particular with each moment, except to be present in it. We came here to experience all the highs and lows, the lefts and rights — to diminish the value of any one moment, forgetting that we understand them best in contrast to each other, would be wasteful indeed. We came here for all of them.

As you see, my communication with Lynne did not exactly entail the back and forth spontaneity of conversation, which is what I suspect Margaret can experience, although she seemed to receive my questions. The information I got was more like receiving a letter or a package, or a download. While I missed the repartee Lynne and I had when she was on this side of the veil, I was happy and grateful to still be able to communicate now that she was on the other.

Sometimes I got a scenario all at one time and sometimes it felt like there was static and it took me a few connections to get the whole story. Overall, her experiences are sequenced here as I received them. I hope you may find them as fascinating as I have.

The Children

One of the first things I'm doing...

I saw a square, white, translucent tube — perfectly vertical and quite long. Later it came to me that the tube may be a way for Lynne to travel through different frequencies without being bothered or distracted along the way, sort of like a commuter train through various dimensions. At the time I didn't think to ask about it, because what I saw next captured my complete attention.

Below the tube there were 12-15 children in robes, milling around. At first I thought they were on an island, then I realized it probably was just a confined space. They seemed to be aged from 3 years to about 16. There was no interaction among them and although they were very close, no one bumped into anyone else. Milling around is the best way to describe their slow, constant meandering.

...is helping these children, who have been so traumatized that their souls are fragmented and chaotic. What I do, one at a time, is energetically bring the parts of their soul together and hold them in place, so they can re-experience and hopefully remember what it's like to feel whole. Then when I slowly let go, they may be able to hold themselves together a little better on their own and won't be quite as fragmented or chaotic as they were — it's a process.

They're not aware that I'm here, they're barely aware of each other. Anything external is very threatening to them, so I will only reveal myself gently after someone has enough cohesion to tolerate it. No one and nothing is forced.

What apparently makes me special at this is that something about my energy is really good "glue" to hold the parts of their souls together. It breaks through their numbness to trigger a spark of awareness, a glimpse of recognition, so they will begin to move toward regaining wholeness themselves as best they can.

I pictured Tom Hanks in *Castaway* rubbing sticks to start a fire and waiting for the spark. Lynne, like a girl-scout, patiently coaxing sparks! And realizing how shut-down these children were, I thought, "I guess there's no talking them out of feeling like victims, is there…?" Clearly, she heard my thought!

Right, ALL they perceive is their victimization. As they recreate a more cohesive identity, they will gradually develop a perception of themselves outside of the trauma, remember who they are. They need to regain a more whole perception of themselves to get out of the victimhood.

I envisioned that from a stain, like a puddle of coffee, there emerged a small, silver-white bit of lining on one edge — that 'other perception of themselves.' Then ever-so-slowly the silver-white area spread across the puddle, so the stain shrank and fell away like a scab. To be able to shed their trauma, each child would have to be able to stand solidly outside of it.

Remembering that in shamanic work, there is a prac-tice called 'soul retrieval' to reintegrate parts of our selves that fragment off or become lost when we experience emotional injury, I asked, "Are all of their soul pieces here now?"

Yes, that has already been done by others. This is my stage of the work.

Reviewing Your Life
There is a sort of guidance council. You go to them when you want and feel ready. No one forces you.

I saw just the angles of a triangle, as if the sides had been erased up to an inch from the points. Tucked inside each of the three angles, like a child's time-out stool placed in a corner, was a light, although no two lights were on at the same time. They blinked slowly at alternating intervals — red, yellow, and blue/green — with no predictable pattern that I noticed. Each light felt sentient, but more like a committee than a single entity.

You stand in the middle. They help you understand yourself better — they expose your underlying beliefs. For example, in your lifetime, you may have felt stuck and blamed your circumstances for not allowing you to do more or be more. What you were not acknowledging is that you believed if you moved forward, you would be leaving someone behind. And that was a situation you would not consciously allow yourself to face.

No one tells you what to do with this information — how to deal with it is up to you. I think they only tell what you're ready to hear. Somehow they read you and are very kind about it; there is no sense of judgment. Like I said, no one and nothing is forced.

Holding an Energy Frequency

I'm meeting people here. When we're not away working on assignments, we tend to congregate. We know that most of us have known each other before, but it takes time to remember where and when — the memories don't flood back all at once. Something will happen or one of us will think about something, and then it triggers more recall. It's like when you recognize someone out of context and can't quite place them, it's just at the edge of your awareness.

We're learning to hold energy. It's like finding the spot in a room where there is a certain temperature. Or following the sound of one instrument in a symphony. Or tracking an aroma. You sense just that particular level or stream of... well, energy, and keep yourself aligned with it. None of the rest of the room or the symphony goes away, it's all there at the same time. But you lock onto the particular vibration you want and sort of ride it.

It doesn't depend on how fast you catch it, but how well you can hold your awareness in that one lane, so to speak, and move into it. Like not falling off a tight-rope, but instead of trying to balance in place, it's like running into it. To you, it would probably be most like trying to hold your mind on a single thought and not let it wander.

Different levels of energy look like different colors to me. I see several distinct colors here where you would barely distinguish one shade from another. Locking onto one color and trying to hold my energy with it feels like squeezing under a closed door — like I said, staying in a narrow lane. Someone else might see these energy lanes like cells on a spread sheet, or dots in a grid pattern. There's no wrong way, just different people see things differently...

At first I was trying to squeeze myself into this narrow space and then I figured out that I could simply widen it with my imagination. Another person might accomplish it by making himself thinner — again, there's no wrong way. I suppose you could imagine it becoming a box and climb in!

This made perfect sense to me because I already believe our imagination is not to be distrusted, but respected. Western education promotes logic over imagination. The way I see things, it may be logic that drives, but it's imagination that navigates.

What's important about this holding energy trick is that it's not just WHAT we do, it's HOW we do things. Over here it's as fundamental as breathing.

Meeting People

I guess I expected that meeting people here would be like meeting people there: when you picture folks in the physical world, what is most notice-able is their appearance, which primarily depends on racial features. Those features are here but they're not primary — what is primary here is a person's awareness or energy frequency.

Outward features mean little here. It's sort of like having shoes to go to a party and leaving them at the door.

I thought this was a pretty funny analogy, since I'd recently returned from helping Lynne's husband go through some of her things and we were surprised to find a few couple hundred pairs of shoes, mostly new in their boxes, stacked at the tops of closets. Who knew Lynne was a shoe person?

She'd always been able to laugh at herself easily. It was good to feel her laugh after I remembered all the boxes we'd found, and hear her say, *And there I was saving all those shoes — for what????*

Teasing Friends

We pulled a pretty good joke on a person here who was working to hold his energy at a particular level, like I explained about isolating a color and riding it. Several of us acted like we weren't even noticing but surrounded him with thoughts of a different energy level. It was just in fun; we didn't do it for very long. And it worked — as a group, we held our energy really well on a frequency just a little off from what he was trying to hold, and surrounded him with it. After awhile he gave up in mild frustration sighing, "No matter how hard I try to get this orange, it keeps coming out too yellow!" We all burst out laughing and said, "Yeah, that's what it looks like to us, too!"

I thought, "Ah Lynnie, still up to your old tricks!" My friend Lynne, you might find interesting, had years before convinced her co-workers in a meeting to try a "really great new hand lotion." She'd made a big deal of how much better it was than other products, "you really have to try this." And once everyone had their hands slathered up, she informed them it was really sexual lubricant!

The Farmer and the Sheep

This segment made sense to me because I'd already heard that our pets often take on ailments in an attempt to show us something we need to pay attention to, or even part of our ailments so we might have less to endure.

I was asked to intercede and help some animals. A farmer had a flock of sheep undergoing an 'event.' They were taking on a muscle disease that advanced slowly but ultimately would cause their deaths. It started in their legs and progressed up into the rest of their bodies. The sheep were voluntarily taking this on as a group agreement to show the farmer that he was not moving forward, that his resistance to something new was preventing him from carrying himself forward in life.

I pictured 30 to 40 sheep who loved this farmer very much, and he loved them in return. More than half of them had various stages of the disabling condition that Lynne described. Initially it symptomized as shakiness in the legs, then led to increasing difficulty in walking, to the point that they would not be able to stand. I'm sure the farmer had been trying to find out what this disease was and how to cure it. When I've told this story at small gatherings, someone recognized this disease one time and named it, but I don't remember what it's called.

Well, the farmer had died and now the sheep were left in the midst of this event. At first I didn't know what to do. So I decided to ask each sheep. I read the energy field of the flock to learn which ones wanted to remain in their bodies and work their way back to health, and which felt they had progressed so far with the disease that they were ready to die. This decision seemed to also tie in with how old a sheep was, in that it may have felt ready to leave on that account. It was important to me to be sure that each sheep had the opportunity to make its own choice.

Once that was determined, I created a wall within their energy field that separated the two sides — those who wanted to live and those who were ready to die. From that I sent a pulse into both groups, which would accelerate their intention. All I really did was make it so the one group would get well faster and the other group would not take as long to die. About two-thirds of the flock remained in good health after that with no residual signs of the disabling condition. To the farmer's family, it just looked like the disease had run its course.

The End
Gradually the emotional portals closed, time between downloads became longer and longer, and the information I received had less clarity. The stories I have after these are fragmented and incomplete.

What I find most satisfying from this information is to understand the kinds of things we can do when we cross over. Years ago, I would wonder, "What's there to DO anything with on the other side, if you don't have hammers, or pencils, or materials and stuff?" Now I understand — it's all energy!

Epilogue

So there you have it — it's all energy! The basis of who we are, even in the body, is energy. Actually I hear there are differences there too, between our spirit and our soul, but for our purposes here I don't think we need to get into that.

What I believe serves us to think about at this point — unless you prefer to eschew the personal accounts herein and that's certainly your prerogative — is how it may behoove us to keep in mind that we are permanent energetic beings having temporary physical experiences. How that perception can influence our interpretation of what occurs in our lives and the decisions we make in response. And how that understanding can support our personal resilience.

As a hypnotherapist, I'm convinced that what happens to us is never as important as what we make of it, and that all healing is a matter of reinterpreting the events that have caused us pain. As you hear more frequently these days: pain is inevitable, suffering is optional.

My own brand of hypnosis is transpersonal, which takes into account that we each are a mind, a body, and a spirit; which purports that within whatever belief system we choose, we can access powerful and positive inner resources; and which furthermore holds that we can be guided by a super-conscious aspect of ourselves to uncover what is in our best interests.

Hopefully you have seen that if you are feeling blocked in some way from your goals, you often will not know why because the root of it is not in your conscious mind. Hopefully, when you're ready, you may also consider getting to know yourself better and trust that your subconscious is still YOU, trying to help but maybe in need of some updates. When you're ready.

Made in the USA
San Bernardino, CA
07 July 2014